EXEMPLARY DAMAGES

By Dennis O'Driscoll

Poetry

KIST

HIDDEN EXTRAS

LONG STORY SHORT

QUALITY TIME

WEATHER PERMITTING

Essays

TROUBLED THOUGHTS, MAJESTIC DREAMS

Dennis O'Driscoll

EXEMPLARY
DAMAGES

ANVIL PRESS POETRY

Published in 2002
by Anvil Press Poetry Ltd
Neptune House 70 Royal Hill London SE10 8RF
Reprinted in 2003
www.anvilpresspoetry.com

This book is published with financial assistance
from The Arts Council of England

Designed and set in Monotype Ehrhardt by Anvil
Printed and bound in England
by Cromwell Press, Trowbridge, Wiltshire

ISBN 0 85646 350 7

A catalogue record for this book
is available from the British Library

FRANK, SEAMUS, MARIE, DECLAN, EITHNE

as it was in the beginning

ACKNOWLEDGEMENTS

Acknowledgements are due to the editors of the following publications in which some of the poems in this collection first appeared: *London Review of Books, Metre, New Hibernia Review, New Statesman, Oxford Magazine, The Paris Review, Poetry Ireland Review, Poetry London, Portal* (EXPO 2000), *The Recorder, The Southern Review, Thumbscrew, Times Literary Supplement* and *TriQuarterly*.

'Tulipomania', 'In Town' and 'Full Flight' were first published in *Poetry* (Chicago). 'A Bowl of Cherries' appeared in English and Flemish in *De Brakke Hond* (Belgium).

Further acknowledgements are made to the anthology, *101 Poems to Get You Through the Day (and Night)*, edited by Daisy Goodwin (HarperCollins, 2000), where 'No, Thanks' appeared; the poem was broadcast on RTE Radio 1. 'Variations on Yellow', commissioned for *A Conversation Piece*, edited by Adrian Rice and Angela Reid (Ulster Museum/Abbey Press, 2002), also appeared in *Patrick Scott: A Retrospective* (Hugh Lane Gallery, 2002) and was broadcast on RTE Radio 1.

For the quotations in 'England' from Stanley Baldwin, John Major and John Betjeman, I am indebted to Jeremy Paxman's *The English* (Michael Joseph, 1998).

Finally and emphatically, a large debt of gratitude is owed to the Lannan Foundation for a Literary Award in 1999.

CONTENTS

Part One

OUT OF CONTROL

Worry on, mothers: you have
good reason to lose sleep,
to let imaginations run riot
as you lie in bed, not counting sheep
but seeing sons and daughters
like lambs led to slaughter
in the road kill of Friday nights.

Remain on standby, mothers –
you never know your luck –
for the knock that would break
the silence like the shock
of a metallic impact against brick.
Keep imagining a police beacon,
a blue moon shattering the darkness.

Lie warily, mothers, where,
eighteen years before, conception
took place in the black of night,
a secret plot; wait restlessly,
as if for a doctor's test,
to find out whether
you are still with child.

HEART TO HEART

Heart, how well we've come
to know one another,
though we've never met.

We are like blood brothers,
pen friends communicating
through bright ink.

'We must arrange a rendezvous',
we say; but the red-letter day
is continually postponed.

Heart, we grew up together –
until, by now, your
walls are plush with fat,

a mud-spattered car after
a long journey – but have
yet to meet in the flesh.

What, I wonder, do you look like?
Those turnip-shaped
ox hearts in butcher shops,

aesthetically aligned
on metal plates, cuddling up
like litters of new pups?

Heart, you stood by me
always, adjusting your beat
as the occasion required,

slowing to a funeral march
or hastening to match the pace
of love's provocations.

We were inseparable when
you took your first sip of blood.
You shared my rapture when,

one magic morning,
plovers rose from fields
like doves from a conjurer's hat.

Heart – pump, sump, soak-pit,
purification station –
keep up the pressure:

fight to the last white
corpuscle, squeeze
the last drop from my life.

BLOOD RELATIONS

I

Who descended from whom.
Who has whose eyes.
Whose nose.
Whose bone marrow matches whose.
Whose blood group.
Viscous as crude oil.
Sticky situations.
Four times thicker than water.
Brought to boiling point
at the least slip of the tongue.

II

Drain the tainted blood
that battles, red-hot,
through your veins,

defended once
in tribal fights
and cattle raids.

Liquidate your
hate-bearing genes:
sterilise them with water

spilt at the sword-point
of a stalactite
in some ancestral cave.

III

Blood is what earns you
a sponsor's place
at the baptismal font
cradling your newest niece;

or, sporting a paper crown,
the right to dish out breast of turkey
at the Christmas get-together,
test the firmness of pink ham;

the privilege to share
in triumph or disgrace,
put up bail, act as guarantor,
face the midnight call.

IV

Cells dunked in plasma,
fruit in syrup.
Clots, blockages, oxygen loss.

Such scope for bad blood.
The potency to pump 8,000 litres in a day.
100,000 beats worth.

More than your hardening
arteries may find
the capacity to forgive.

HIGH SPIRITS

Knowing time is not on their side, the old make no bones
about enjoying a night life, catching up, scraping the best
from the years that are left; sneaking out while households sleep –
2 a.m. or 3 – under a moon draped with loose-fitting clouds
like a pale grandmother dwarfed by her dressing gown.

There is safety in numbers for the old; but the young,
returning home in disco fashions or long satin debs gowns
are repulsed, disgusted by the withered skin-flaps
shamelessly exposed through low-cut nightdresses,
pyjama stripes clashing with tartan bedroom slippers.

A man stops suddenly, starts, laughs hysterically, whispers
confidentially in a wispy voice; a shrieking woman beats
on the laundrette window, demanding a pennyworth of sweets.
Another seeks directions to the teacher's house from no one:
she must hand in homework before her birthday party begins.

The high spirits of the old provoke pandemonium.
Boosting the decibel levels, their sons and daughters
cause a traffic snarl-up, waiting to cruise dawn streets
for straying parents whom they will find blissfully happy
though suspicious of the strangers offering them a lift:

a parent who has no reason to miss his spouse, since she
is not dead – just temporarily mislaid like house keys;
a parent without a worry in the world, unless you count
an anxiety to check that her shoes are still snug in the fridge,
her infant son with chicken pox still sleeping soundly in the box
    room.

CLINICAL ELATION

I

In the out-patients' cubicle,
  you shed the paper gown
and dive, head-first, for cover –
shirt and sweater – relieved
your sentence is deferred.
Reprieved, you melt back
    into the city crowd, the rush-hour
    cortège of cars unmoved for miles.

How fresh this stale world seems:
  like the aniseed smell of wildflowers;
sweet globes of pineapple-weed squeezed
between fingers on a riverbank
from which supple trout are spotted
fluttering in pools, then glossing
    over moss and stone, a pianist's
    hands angling for glissando notes.

II

You are in your stride now,
  in denial, walking away from trouble,
elated as a child catching a first dramatic
glance of the flickering wide-screen sea
behind guest houses with *No Vacancies*,
rest homes for retirees, souvenir shops
    gritted with sand – spades and windmills,
    tubes and water-wings displayed outside.

Then the huge expanse of unimpeded
ocean leached through hazy light;
one right turn more grants barefoot access.
The family car brakes – like a beached
wave – to a halt: the scene compressed
into perspective from a dune top
but stopping at nothing, hinting
at the infinity you race towards.

SATURDAY NIGHT FEVER

Playing tonight at the X-Ray-Ted Club,
The Chemotherapies, drugged to the gills,
the lead singer's pate modishly bald.

And who will your partner be?
Alzheimer, the absent-minded type,
with the retro gear, everything a perfect mismatch?

Huntington, grooving his hippy-hippy-shake routine?
Thrombosis, the silly clot, trying to pull a stroke?
Angina, who can be such a pain, and yet is all heart?

Raynaud, decked in ice-blue, coolest kid around?
Dear sweet Emphysema, so exercised she hardly
has a chance to catch her second wind?

Cancer, the rogue, ever-gregarious, spreading himself
around, groping his way niftily to a breast?
Parkinson who is already restless for the next number?

They sweat it out all night under the lightning strikes
of strobe lights flashing like an ambulance – such fun
that nobody, as they groan with pleasure, dreams of sleep.

YEARS AFTER

And yet we managed fine.

We missed your baking for a time.
And yet were we not better off
without cream-hearted sponge cakes,
flaky, rhubarb-oozing pies?

Linoleum-tiled rooms could no longer
presume on your thoroughgoing scrub;
and yet we made up for our neglect,
laid hardwood timber floors.

Windows shimmered less often.
And yet we got around to
elbow-greasing them eventually.
Your daily sheet-and-blanket

rituals of bedmaking were more
than we could hope to emulate.
And yet the duvets we bought
brought us gradually to sleep.

Declan and Eithne (eleven
and nine respectively at the time)
had to survive without your packed
banana sandwiches, wooden spoon

deterrent, hugs, multivitamins.
And yet they both grew strong:
you have unmet grandchildren,
in-laws you never knew.

Yes, we managed fine, made
breakfasts and made love,
took on jobs and mortgages,
set ourselves up for life.

And yet. And yet. And yet.

EXEMPLARY DAMAGES

I

What are humans for?
To set a pace that ensures
the question will never arise?
To mortify the flesh
in a slum sweat shop

or build up a portfolio
of dot com shares?
To pare the nails of a wasted
hospice patient or to ward off
evil with a fighter plane?

To pay lip service to a life
that is always losing face,
as we gauge the state
of our souls in the mirror's
cold sores, sallow skin?

What are we made for?
To live and let live?
To give and take?
To survive the dark night of the soul?
To make more of ourselves?

II

Our one true God has died, vanished under
a rainbow's arch, banished like a devil
scalded by holy water; but our lives remain
eternally precious in the eyes of man.

We love one another so much the slightest
hurt cries out for compensation: sprain your
ankle in a pothole and City Hall will pay
exemplary damages for your pains;

we are equal under law as we once were
in His sight – just as He kept tabs
on the hairs of our heads, the sparrows
surfing the air, we are all accounted for,

enshrined in police department databases,
our good names maintained by the recording
angels of mailshot sales campaigns,
rewarded with chainstore loyalty points.

III

The baby is at the end
of its umbilical tether, awaiting delivery,
bubble-wrapped in an amniotic sac.

The doctor is alert
to every knock the foetal heartbeat makes
at the womb's front door.

The father has bought
a cellophane-sheathed baby seat
for installation in the family car.

The mother is ready
to stifle cries of distress
at the wellhead of her breast.

Wool blankets to hand,
they are all on standby
like a search and rescue party

keeping vigil near a cave.

IV

How will there ever be goods enough, white goods,
dry goods, grave goods, munitions, comestibles,
to do justice to all the peoples of the world?

Enough parma ham, however thinly curled,
to serve with cottage cheese and chives
in the cavernous canteens of high-rise buildings?

Enough rubs and creams, suppositories and smears,
mesh tops and halter necks, opaques and sheers?
How will there ever be enough flax steeped for smart

linen suits, enough sheep shorn for lambswool coats,
enough goats for cashmere stoles to wear on opening nights,
enough cotton yarn to spin into couture tops, flak jackets?

And can we go on satisfying orders for baseball caps, chicken
        nuggets,
body toning pads, lotion for chapped lips? And what quantity
of dolphin-friendly skipjack tuna meets a sushi bar's demands?

And how much serviced land remains for leisure-centre
        building,
how much hardwood forest has been cleared for grazing,
        how many
quarries can still serve as landfill sites for agribusiness waste?

And will there be sufficient creatures left to brighten up
our morning drives with road kill? Will the fox's brush-fire
be extinguished, the hedgehog's yard-brush be swept aside?

What hope of raw ingredients for peroxide bleach, wheelie
        bins,
beach thongs, gluten-free bread, protective welding masks,
trucks transporting cars like reptiles ferrying their young?

V

Let's call it a day, abandon
the entire perverted experiment,
refuse to collude any longer with
the crude manipulations of sex,
the need for extra housing stock,
the record pressures on hospital beds.

Scrap the misbegotten concept
altogether, let the noxious rivers
wind their serpentine way towards
the caesium-fished, oil-slicked sea,
the stores of nerve gas escape
through the widening ozone hole.

Burn the lot, the speculative rot propagated
about extra-terrestrial intelligence,
the self-help books to combat fear and stress,
the rules for ethical genetic engineering,
the blunt facts about cloning, the Bible tracts,
the glib self-deceptive upbeat texts.

Take it away, the latest theory on
bowel cancer and stem cell research.
Tear from limb to limb the handbook
on palliative care with its matter-of-fact
chapters on genitourinary disorders,
charts for accurate measurement of pain.

Let's not bestir ourselves to purge
the unholy mess, our daily urge to dispose
of rosy tampons, soiled baby Pampers,
home-delivery pizza styrofoam,
the hardening mustard crust of sewage,
thirst-quenching diet Pepsi cans.

It was all destined to end badly, near
the reactor core; or at the city dump
where fridges pour out their gaseous souls
and black plastic sacks spill synthetic
viscera for pillaging shanty dwellers
to scavenge, reap what we have sown.

VI

At the far end of the day
        you feel compelled
to lay down your head:
        an earthenware pitcher.
And it's a wonder
        you can contain all
you bottle up inside:
        enough to breach
the skull's crust, shift
        its hairline cracks,
disturb tectonic plates.

MISSING GOD

His grace is no longer called for
before meals: farmed fish multiply
without His intercession.
Bread production rises through
disease-resistant grains devised
scientifically to mitigate His faults.

Yet, though we rebelled against Him
like adolescents, uplifted to see
an oppressive father banished –
a bearded hermit – to the desert,
we confess to missing Him at times.

Miss Him during the civil wedding
when, at the blossomy altar
of the registrar's desk, we wait in vain
to be fed a line containing words
like 'everlasting' and 'divine'.

Miss Him when the TV scientist
explains the cosmos through equations,
leaving our planet to revolve on its axis
aimlessly, a wheel skidding in snow.

Miss Him when the radio catches a snatch
of plainchant from some echoey priory;
when the gospel choir raises its collective voice
to ask *Shall We Gather at the River?*
or the forces of the oratorio converge
on *I Know That My Redeemer Liveth*
and our contracted hearts lose a beat.

Miss Him when a choked voice at
the crematorium recites the poem
about fearing no more the heat of the sun.

Miss Him when we stand in judgement
on a lank Crucifixion in an art museum,
its stripe-like ribs testifying to rank.

Miss Him when the gamma-rays
recorded on the satellite graph
seem arranged into a celestial score,
the music of the spheres,
the *Ave Verum Corpus* of the observatory lab.

Miss Him when we stumble on the breast lump
for the first time and an involuntary prayer
escapes our lips; when a shadow crosses
our bodies on an x-ray screen; when we receive
a transfusion of foaming blood
sacrificed anonymously to save life.

Miss Him when we call out His name
spontaneously in awe or anger
as a woman in the birth ward bawls
her long-dead mother's name.

Miss Him when the linen-covered
dining table holds warm bread rolls,
shiny glasses of red wine.

Miss Him when a dove swoops
from the orange grove in a tourist village
just as the monastery bell begins to take its toll.

Miss Him when our journey leads us
under leaves of Gothic tracery, an arch
of overlapping branches that meet
like hands in Michelangelo's creation.

Miss Him when, trudging past a church,
we catch a residual blast of incense,
a perfume on par with the fresh-baked loaf
which Milosz compared to happiness.

Miss Him when our newly-decorated kitchen
comes in Shaker-style and we order
a matching set of Mother Ann Lee chairs.

Miss Him when we listen to the prophecy
of astronomers that the visible galaxies
will recede as the universe expands.

Miss Him the way an uncoupled glider
riding the evening thermals misses its tug.

Miss Him, as the lovers shrugging
shoulders outside the cheap hotel
ponder what their next move should be.

Even feel nostalgic, odd days,
for His Second Coming,
like standing in the brick
dome of a dovecote
after the birds have flown.

Part Two

CALLING THE KETTLE

No matter what news breaks,
it's impossible to think straight
until the kettle has been boiled.

The kettle with its metal back
strong enough to take the strain,
shoulders broad enough to cry on;

plump as the old grandmother
in her woollen layers of skirts
who is beyond surprise or shock,

who knows the value of allowing
tears to flow, of letting off steam,
of wetting the tea and, her hand

patting your cheek, insisting – as she
prevails on you to sit and drink – that
things could have been much worse.

HEAT WAVE

Heat brought the day to its senses.
We are not used to such direct
expressions of feeling here
with our wishy-washy weather,
our dry intervals and showers,

our clearance spreading from the west;
rain and shine – ham actors –
mixing up their lines.
But there it was, the real thing,
an unstinting summer day,

not rationing its latitude for heat,
not squeezing out its precious metal
meanly between cracks in cloud.
Sunflower dishes tracked a solar path
across the radar screen of sky.

Apples swelled but still fell
short of breaking point.
The taut skin of black currants
would spurt open at a touch.
Ripening grain was hoarded

in the aprons of corn stalks.
A bee paused as if to dab its brow,
before lapping up more gold reserves.
Tar splashed the ankles of cars
as they negotiated honey-sticky routes.

Foxglove, ox-eyed daisy, vetch
jostled for attention on the verges.
Spiders hung flies out to dry.

A coiled snake – puff adder
or reticulated python – would

have thrived in that environment,
peaches supplanting gooseberries.
Were the river not reduced
to a trickle of juice within
reed-bearded banks, it might

have furnished cover for a crocodile
with sloped back patterned
like heat-soaked patio bricks.
A sudden low-lying cat dashed
between houses like a cheetah.

If that sun had made itself heard
it would have sounded like the inner
ferment of a cask of vintage wine,
the static on a trunk-call line
when someone phones out of the blue . . .

Birds retreated into silence, perched
deep inside leaf-camouflaged trees,
having nothing meaningful to add,
no dry-throated chalk-screeching
jungle note that would fit the bill.

A day that will spell summer always
for the child, too young to speak,
who romped outside among flower beds,
his mother's voice pressed thin and flat
as she summoned him languidly back

to the cool, flagstoned kitchen,
ice-cream blotches daubed
like sun block on his pudgy face.

A BOWL OF CHERRIES

for Pat Morrison

I

While, granted, life may not be
a bowl of cherries on the whole,
Osias Beert gave literal expression
to the more upbeat view in his
sixteen hundred and something
painting, *Still Life with Cherries.*
Its glow – a wood-burning stove –
caught my eye in Stockholm
one harbour-stiffening winter.
Long-spired churches sniffed
the icy air; berries were served
on branches like arctic cherries.
Silhouetted pine trees shivered;
their saw-toothed outlines
chattered in raw snow.

II

Although the season of cherries
is brief, the painter set aside
his griefs to let joy have its way,
each puff-cheeked fruit in its first
flush of youth, a trumpet-blowing
cherub; the roe of some exotic
species plucked from juice, not brine;
the rods and cones of the sun's eye.

The painter's plate is full now
and he is satisfied with his lot
even if the rot will set in soon
and the freshness is pure deception
lasting no longer than cherry blossoms
tossed on snow when north winds
are enjoying their final fling.

III

There are times, his painting
seems to say – and this is one
of them – when, despite all
evidence to the contrary, life is
(and no denying it) a bowl of cherries.
Just look at this picture: so rich a crop
that some have dropped off the edge
like coins spilt from a collection plate.
And, though Osias may be far off
the mark where truth (whatever
about beauty) is concerned,
the cherries – bite-size apples –
tempt with their own improbable
knowledge and the cold viewer's
eyes helplessly assent.

TULIPOMANIA

And who on earth would blame them,
those Dutch merchants prepared
to give up everything they owned
for the pearl of great price
that is a tulip bulb?

What house wallowing in canal mud,
like a rigged-out ship marooned
in harbour, could hold its own,
however secure its moorings,
against the ground-breaking tulip egg
that incubates in spring, sprouting shoots
of incandescent plumage: tangerine feathers
rippled with pink, streaked with aquamarine?

And who, with his priorities in place,
would hesitate to exchange
his very home for the tulip that leaves
no blood-red trail of perfume
but proceeds to make its bed
in the tactile gloss of satin sheets?

What crinoline gown, what silk
chemise, slithering to the boards
of a lead-windowed bedroom,
could compare with this stranger
bearing arcane knowledge from
a stream-splashed crag in Tien Shan
or the snow-melts of Tashkent?

Who wouldn't want to fade out
in a blaze of glory? Who wouldn't
sacrifice himself on an altar
of urn-shaped tulips, a pyre
of flaming crimsons, smoky maroons?

Who wouldn't be the better
for the lesson of those petals,
dropping off like share values,
precious metal rates,
leaving time to meditate on fortune,
speculate on loss?

LOVE LIFE

You really have to hand it to them.
They let nothing stand between them
and love's work; even in the face
of inequality and AIDS, admit
no impediment that would detract
from glossy theories of attraction
(*Put your seduction skills to the test
with this month's questionnaire . . .*),
'love' and 'forever' sharing the one
sentence like a king-size bed.

You really have to marvel at men
chivalrous enough to let themselves
be mesmerised by model bodies
conjured up on websites,
at women brushing up techniques
to keep their men on side,
despite courtroom reports
of barring orders, statistics
for divorce, incompatibility
on housework rotas, sport.

You have to recognise
the nobility in this busy,
cost-effective era of devoting
tranches of scarce time resources
to nail-painting, e-mail vigils,
rose bouquets, singles dinners,
basement bars, lace uplift bras,
discounting the mounting evidence
of chins, thinning crowns, downward
projections for the future.

You have to concede the idealism
it takes to get dressed up
to impress, then divest each other
of glad rags, down to the last
sad tufts of private hair; in an age
of hygiene hyper-awareness
to allow tongues explore where they will
as the muscular grip of the heart
tightens with excitement, a breaking
bag of waters ready to let rip.

Miraculous how the old ways survive:
gazing into another's eyes like precious
stones – spurning scientific findings
about hormones, seminal vesicles,
gametogenesis, selfish genes.
Voices dim, discreet as recessed
lights, over a bistro meal;
aired confidences, bared souls;
fingertips meet on the wine-stained
gingham cloth, feet entwine.

And so a new generation comes round
to the problem pages of teen magazines,
mastering the body-language needed
for hanging out at shopping mall
McDonald's or music megastore,
navels pierced, tiny skirts and shiny
cropped tops sneaked to weekend clubs,
unknown to parents offered curt
assurances about who'll be where
tonight, who with, till when . . .

And so your grandparents' names
are back in fashion, your twinkly
grandparents by whom the word 'sex'
was never expressed in your hearing,

whom you could never remotely imagine
making what we now call love.
'Still going on', as the great,
supposedly fouled-up Philip Larkin
(in an entirely different context)
wrote, 'all of it, still going on!'

THE LADS

Technicians, overseers, assistant
depot managers, stock controllers.
Old fashioned nine-to-five men
who rose moderately up the line.
You can pick them out in tea break
identity parades at the Quick Snack
café, bellies extending under
diamond-patterned sweaters.

They tuck into a fry – it's pay day,
after all, a day of their lives,
and their wives, a bit too fond
of calorie counting, restrict
fry-ups now to Christmas,
the odd holiday B & B.

The lads still flirt, as readily
as the next man, with the waitress
and break into synchronised grins
at her snappy repartee.
But it's mainly sport the talk
embraces these times, though
their playing days are over,
apart from the veterans' league,
a pre-pub Sunday game
of pitch-and-putt.

That there are worse fates
they know well enough;
and who'd want to be
among those bosses
monotonously talking shop?
Not for all the BMWs
in the world would they swap.

One of the lads takes to the idea
of early retirement with a convert's zeal.
Not that he feels old or anything –
never felt better, in fact, give or take
the back complaint, his smoker's hack . . .
It's just that the kids have gone
their own strong-willed ways
and the wife works part-time
in the plastics factory crèche.

Before the lads pocket
their hands, stand up to go,
they check their lotto numbers,
bantering about the jet they'll charter
to Thailand when their syndicate wins.

Nibble on a bacon rind
discarded on the mopped-up plate.
Life tastes great some days.

THE CLERICALS

How slowly, in those pre-flexi days, the cautious hands
of standard-issue civil service clocks moved, leaving you
impatient to change into flowered polyester frocks,
cheesecloth skirts, bellbottoms, platform shoes,
finding the sequinned night still young at 2 a.m.,
held in its velvet embrace under the gaze
of a ballroom's crystal moon, a disco's excitable lights.

Marys, Madges, Kathleens, it seems an age
since you guarded public hatches or sat in cream
and mildew-green gloss-painted offices, updating
records, typing carbon-copy letters on demand
for bosses, serving them leaf tea, checking the tot-ups
for payment warrants on slim adding-machine rolls,
date-stamping in-tray correspondence, numbering files.

The years have not been at all kind to you.
Your lives have not withstood the test of time:
not a spare cardigan draped on a chair-back,
not a card-index, not a hard-copy file remains
from the glory days of 1970-whatever when
your generation held the monopoly on being young:
twenty-firsts, all-night parties in a friend's friend's flat . . .

Your youth was snatched from your nail-varnished grasp,
lasting no longer than the push-button hall lights in red-brick
houses where you returned by taxi in a pay-day's early hours,
barely allowed time to step inside and locate your bedsit key
before the darkness resumed: you unlocked the warped
plywood door in the eerie silence of a sleeping corridor,
set the fluorescent alarm clock on the prowl for morning,

undressed, flopped on the foam mattress, dreamt.

FULL FLIGHT

I

Vapour trails:
worm casts left
by burrowing planes;

a wake of surf
on the shipping lanes
of an inverted sea;

pink streaks squirted
at dawn from an aerosol can;
straight lines drawn

by an unsteady hand;
wing tracks rutting
flight paths.

II

All eyes on the annunciator screen, families
locate their check-in bay, before passing through
the x-ray vetting and the plexiglas walkway
to lounge around Departures, dressed in loud
anticipation of another climate, the blow-dry hot-air
blast that will greet them on arrival like a tour guide.

Boarding, in row-order, is called for raucously
at last; carry-on bags are manoeuvred into
narrow bins or stored discreetly under seats,
duty-free vodka bottles jangling like foreign coins.
Belts snap shut, cameras are flashed, blockbusters
deposited on laps, children plied with puzzle books.

The in-flight magazine is yanked from its
elasticated pocket; newspaper readers settle
on sports; business-class curtains close ranks;
a mix-up in a seat allotment is resolved.
Film themes and jazzed-up classics serve
as ambient music, the plane swerving into action.

Mist lifts from runway grass; a wedge
of leftover moon nestles on a shelf of cloud.
Engines gather the reckless speed
needed to raise wings to a higher plane,
to take off from the long flight path
of the tarmac, a dead-end country lane.

Below the dimmed cabin, a miniature
world – every detail faithfully reproduced –
can now be spied: rivers slop out into the tide;
lakes are potholes gouged in buckled mountains.
Then the land draws a borderline in sand.
Out on a limb, dangling over water,

nothing is seen except waves shuffling
their packs, the metallic dazzle of sea
like the video screens – as yet blank –
on which in-flight movies will be viewed.
The cabin crew, patrolling their beat, smile.
Passengers relax, take the weight off their feet.

III

Arms outstretched,
sunbather on an inflated bed,

the overhead jet
is just that interval

from take-off at which
the stewardess announces

We shall shortly be commencing
our in-flight cabin service.

It might equally be
a speeded-up version

of Bede's fable:
a mechanical sparrow

hightailing it above
that transient banquet hall.

IV

From there, the world is recreated as collage:
waves like a cancelled air mail letter
the artist includes for its ethereal blues.

Then inland over glued-on fields:
wheat a yellowing newspaper page,
furrows the strings of a Picasso guitar.

V

Casting cloud aside
     like passive smoke,
the descending plane
     dips to an elevation
where the Atlantic's
     chop-and-change
is witnessed from
     the safe distance
of a window seat's
     reviewing stand,
a gold coast of sand
     outlined by yellow
highlighter pen:
     stepped waves,
boats towing
     trails of foam.
Then tufted fields
     crop up; wheels
put out feelers,
     anxious to
touch down
     on solid ground.

VI

Having retrieved their sliding cases from the carousel,
they leave the steel-clad baggage hall, declaring nothing,
follow trolleys to where tanned holiday rep,
regional HQ driver or exiled daughter waits;

then proceed beyond car rental stands,
tourist reservation booths, bureaux de change,
out into the shock of open air, the stink
of kerosene, the racket of taxis echoing

through the underpass, of courtesy coaches,
terminal shuttles . . . They have arrived.
Ears still popping, they make small talk,
unzip a purse or money-belt for local bills.

Now they are part of the ring-road traffic
they had pitied from the air, barely moving,
cogs in concrete wheels, passing vast hangars,
double-glazed houses devalued by flight-path noise.

Sheraton registers its name repeatedly in neon:
inside, uniformed crews are allocated rooms;
a bleary wayfarer, all the day's connections missed,
checks in for sleep. Travellers go on being routed,

defying laws of gravity, the risks of law-defying
hijackers, of pilot error, radar failure, lightning storms,
metal fatigue, having confirmed their ETA by air-phone
to grounded office colleague, lover, spouse.

VARIATIONS ON YELLOW

[Yellow Device *by Patrick Scott, Ulster Museum*]

Sun brushes the mountain
before landing on a field
      so lush with buttercups
      they might yield
a painter's yellow pigment
or be cultivated as a cash crop.

*

What does it say of nature's taste
that its décor of choice for waste ground
is invariably the common or garden dandelion,
its over-egged yellow such a flashy colour
to splash out on, compared, say, to the subtle
primrose with its beeswax glow of light?

*

    The swelling yellow sun of early May lures you
westwards again: a country bolt-hole, weekend hideout,
lakeside shack, some perch you can escape to,
      draw back creaking shutters, air out dusty rooms.

*

The relief when a cloud,
        eclipsing the sun, steps out of the light
and fishermen in yellow oilskins
        glisten like the yolk of a guillemot's egg.
A kittiwake takes the plunge, snatches
        a slapstick fish clear of the waves.
It's anyone's guess what may happen next.

                        *

You want to hang on for as long as this
yellow painting radiates illumination,
the way someone in a lunch-break
music shop hesitates to walk out
on a mezzo in full flow: you'd like
that light to shadow you down
the street, pursue you to your desk.

IN TOWN

The wizened country woman
with smoke-tanned skin
is foraging for provisions
among supermarket shelves.

Her floral headscarf is
as broad as it is long,
her fur-trimmed coat
a hand-me-down,

brown bootees patched,
the bag with her
pension money
darned at the strap.

When she pays
at the checkout
for oat flakes, stock
cubes, baking soda,

a cake jammed
inside pink icing,
she is ready for home,
all set for her cottage

along a back-road
that hedges its bets
between the clapped-out
sandpit and the handball alley.

A crocked Ford car,
abandoned by her son,
waits faithfully on
its pedestal of blocks.

Her sheepdog noses weeds
like an ant-eater
or snaps at a passing tractor
to speed it on its way.

Lean cows graze nearby:
udder bells – wind
chimes – brush against
rushes, wildflowers.

Thistles burst open
like worn sofas,
their downy stuffing
puffs and blows.

She keeps a holy water
font topped up, a gleaming
set of willow pattern,
a leatherette car seat

to put visitors at ease,
enough dry peat to see
her comfortably through
an average winter.

She is on her bike now,
the talon of the carrier
safeguarding her groceries
in an iron grip.

REMAINDERS

The street seller of newspapers
is growing old.
One glance and you can tell
that a lifetime of violence
has taken its toll.

War and murder have been
meat and drink to him.
Think of all the catastrophic news
of which he has been the bearer,
all the sensational headlines

he has put through his hands,
all the scandal he has spread,
all the famous dead of whom
his tabloids have spoken badly.
At day's end, when he checks

how many papers are left,
he counts them pensively,
as if preparing a defence,
as if each were a year for which
he simply cannot account.

THRUSH AND ANTI-THRUSH

Definitely not, in the thrush's case,
a matter of fine feathers making
fine birds; yet its speckles lure the eye.
Jumpy also, a tad insecure,
walking with a sack-race hop,
legs propped at an awkward angle
like a dodgy bracket on a home-built shelf.

The brown wings and crown
are its least attractive features
by a fairly long shot,
bringing to mind musty smells
and past their sell-by-date
mushrooms, festering brain-dead
in the vegetable drawer.

Marks should be deducted too
(purely on lapse-of-taste grounds)
for its liposuction diet of flabby snails;
insects picked like scabs from walls;
rubber-band worms coiled round its snout,
gormandised the way the Dutch toss
pickled herrings down the hatch.

Enough rubbish you'd assume to choke
the drains of any gullet, until you catch
the rapturous return journey of song:
rococo notes that cry out for transcribing
on calf parchment with a calligraphy quill –
the opposite of magpies which, for all
their preening, can't rustle up a note

between them, scraping the barrels
of their rapid-fire throats;
pointedly attired in well-pressed
morning suits, though lacking in finesse,
rattling on about nothing,
jarring like a car struggling
to start, the ignition failing to engage.

But it's the thrush's tune
the light expires to, day slipping
through the gnarly fingers of old trees;
a music inducing the absurd spectacle
of a man (myself, say) looking to a bird,
of all things, in a digital epoch,
for entertainment, maybe even truth.

WHILE STOCKS LAST

As long as a blackbird
still mounts the podium
of the aspen tree, making
an impassioned plea for song.

As long as blue tits, painted
like endangered tribesmen,
survive in their rain-forest
of soaking larch.

As long as the trilling lasts
above the office car park
and hands tingle to inscribe
in the margins of buff files,

'The skywriting of a bird
is more permanent than ink'
or 'The robin's eagle eye
questions these projections.'

ENGLAND

'Without nostalgia who could love England?'
— ANNE STEVENSON

Somewhere out there, England lingers
under the bushy brow of thatch that juts
above half-timbered houses in Home Counties.
A mill village survives where a raft
of flag irises rises near the grain loft
and the vicarage garden party is tastefully
announced on a hand-painted sign.
A family pile in Queen Anne style,
available at a knock-down price,
catches the needle-sharp eye
of a Lloyd's 'name' in the auction pages
of *The Field* or *Country Life*.
The hand-crafted. The home-made. The family-run.
Pink briar roses sink their claws
– like painted nails – into the gable walls
of listed cottages at Winchelsea and Rye.
Jersey cream dissolves in steaming scones
at the Salvation Army cake sale.
A smell of new-mown hay, of boiling jam,
of hops vented through an oast house cowl.

England is still out there somewhere,
an owl roosting in an abandoned barn.
You can overhear a pub argument about
the best brew of beer, best-ever shepherd's pie.
Alistair Cooke is delivering his four millionth
'Letter from America'; so many record-breaking
West End performances of 'The Mousetrap' or 'Cats';
the ten thousandth revival of 'An Inspector Calls'.
Tin-plate, ration-coupon laughter from the audience
of a radio panel show; Lillibulero marching

on the BBC World Service, Big Ben chiming
to the second with the tea-time news,
the sig tune for 'Coronation Street' a national anthem.
Johnners greets listeners from Lords
as sunlight is rolled out along striped grass.
The tabloids have murder in their hearts.
That and exclusive photos of the latest
female tennis sensation at wet Wimbledon.
Scoreless draws in the Premier League.
Soft going at Newbury and Kempton Park.
Rain stopping play at a county cricket fixture.

Pastel-painted timber seaside chalets.
Miles of white clifftop caravans like dumped fridges.
A day-trip across ridged Channel waves:
cheap pints of bitter in the car ferry bar,
chips with everything in the cafeteria.
English Breakfast Served All Day in Calais.
Vera Lynn. VE celebrations. Our finest hour.
Poppy wreaths, brittle as old majors'
bones, wilt beneath the stony-faced
gaze of the Great War memorial.
Shakespeare settings by Roger Quilter
and Gerald Finzi in aid of the church tower
restoration fund, the vicar's wife doing
the page-turning needful for the accompanist.
A few tremble-lipped parishioners, feeling
their age, clear throats as the harmonium
is tuned and lend their bronchial best
to 'The Day Thou Gavest, Lord, is Ended'
while watery light through leaded glass
lands, like a housefly, on the brass plate
commemorating the valiant dead of Ladysmith.
Elgar's 'Pomp and Circumstance' arranged
for the Queen's visit by the colliery band.
Ralph Vaughan Williams's 'The Lark Ascending'

in rehearsal at the Free Trade Hall.
Gurney's Severn mists, Housman's blue
remembered hills, Hardy's wind and rain.
A Wilfred Owen troop train falling silent
at an unscheduled stop; or Edward Thomas's
halting express at Adlestrop taking on board
a consignment of pre-war blackbird song.
A brawny chestnut shields the clover-fattened
cattle in a hedgerowed field from searing noon.
Water-colour enthusiasts choose the ideal
viewing point to capture the flamboyant sunset.

The quiet courtesies. The moderation.
The pained smiles. Things left unsaid;
passed over in silence, an unwritten constitution.
Miles of graffitied tower blocks, near treeless
motorways as wide as triumphal boulevards.
Race riots in Brixton and the North.
The peal of street-pleasing steel bands at Notting Hill.
Allotment cabbages with gaping caterpillar wounds.
Words like *tavern* and *shires* and *lea*.
Blazered Henley. Top-hatted Ascot.
Black herringbone for the Royal enclosure.
The wine-jacketed coach driver pointing
his blue-rinse passengers to the loos.
A single-room supplement for Christmas
at a refurbished Grand Hotel in some down-at-heel,
sea-eroded, once-genteel Edwardian town.

Romantic England is neither dead nor gone,
nor with Olivier in the grave.
It is out there somewhere still; plain-speaking
Stanley Baldwin's 'corncrake on a dewy morning,
the sound of the scythe against the whetstone . . .
a plough team coming over the brow of a hill'.
Homely John Major's England still holds its own

somewhere: 'long shadows on county grounds,
warm beer, invincible green suburbs, dog lovers'.
Goodly, portly Sir John Betjeman envisions his England:
'oil-lit churches, Women's Institutes, modest
village inns . . . mowing machines on Saturday afternoons'.

It is somewhere at the back of the mind,
like the back of a newsagent's where plug
tobacco is sold; shining like the polished
skin of a Ribston Pippin or Worcester Pearmain.
It preys on imagination, like pleated ladies
sporting on bowling lawns, like jowelled men
of substance nursing claret in oak-panelled
smoking rooms of jovial private clubs.
See it all for yourself – the quadrangled choir school,
the parterred garden with the honesty box,
the fox-hunting colonel on his high horse,
the Gothic Revival haunt leading through
a topiary arch to gazebo, yew maze,
pet cemetery – on your jaunts through
cobbled market towns, treks down lanes
rutted with what surely must be haywain wheels.

Listen to England as it thunders from Pennine becks
like a loud speech heckled by a Hyde Park crowd.
Listen to its screaming day traders, its bingo callers,
its Speaker demanding 'Order!' in the lower chamber.
Listen to the big band music to which couples
relax at the Conservative Club dinner dance.
Listen to the wax of silence harden
round the red leatherette upholstery
after closing time at the Crown and Rose;
steel shutters come down hard on the Punjab Balti;
grease congeals on the mobile kebab stall.
Listen to the tick of its Town Hall clocks,
like the drip-drying of a Marks and Spencer shirt

hung above a chipped enamel bath.
Listen to the silence in which England finds its voice.
It declaims this sceptered isle, this earth of majesty.
It claims some corner of a foreign field.
It chants while the chaffinch sings on the orchard bough.
It chants history is now and England.
It pleads green and pleasant land.
It pleads for all its many faults.

LAST WORDS

What an absolute creep
Philip Larkin
seems to have been.

Have you read
the letters yet?
The biography?

Did you watch
the tele-prof
cut him down to size?

And, true to form,
he proved a sleazy
bastard to the last:

as he was dying,
he squeezed his
nurse's hand

(she should,
strictly speaking,
have ordered

him to keep
his filthy paws
to himself),

while he croaked
as best the
throat cancer

(which he'd brought
on himself with
smokes and booze)

allowed: *I am going
to the inevitable.*
So negative always.

So obsessed with death.
1.24 a.m., the time.
Except for the nurse,

he was alone – no
visitors, of course,
at that unearthly hour;

no wife or kids
to line up tearfully
around the single bed.

A selfish swine
without doubt;
and, by all accounts,

no great loss.

WAR POET

There is talk of a ceasefire but the poet will hear none of it. If a lasting peace in that distant, barbaric land is really on the cards, he's damned if it will happen until his poem is complete. Only this morning, he felt another surge of inspiration. Images inundate his mind: a bomber plane budding with engines; a wounded man whose guts jut out like the service shafts of the Pompidou Centre . . .

His will be the war poem to end all war poems. A sure-fire competition winner. Now suddenly this premature bullshit about peace: intermediaries, UN envoys, neutral venues, exploratory talks. How can they do this to his poem, before it's had a chance to speak its lines, to influence the outcome of the war? Can the TV bulletins of scorched gables, camps of toothless refugees, famished children – the very scenes that triggered off his poem's wrath – not hold out for a short while more?

But there's hope yet. Negotiations may collapse. Hardline factions may refuse to sign up to the deal. Splinter groups may form. He feels a little steadier. Yes, he'll knock that poem into final shape if it kills him. He will live to see it carved, an eternal flame of words, in the marble columns of a solemn war memorial. The opening stanza – perhaps misquoted slightly – will be publicly trumpeted on commemoration days.

He fumbles for a cigarette, paces his balcony at the sylvan writers' retreat. His morale is on the rise. He knows in his bones the war will – *must* – go on.

NO, THANKS

No, I don't want to drop over for a meal
    on my way home from work.
No, I'd much prefer you didn't feel obliged
    to honour me by crashing overnight.
No, I haven't the slightest curiosity about seeing
    how your attic conversion finally turned out.
No, I'm not the least bit interested to hear
    the low-down on your Florida holiday.
No way am I going to blow a Friday night's freedom
    just to round out numbers at your dinner table.
No, I'm simply not able for the excitement
    of your school-term coffee mornings.
No, strange though it may seem, your dream kitchen
    holds no fascination whatsoever for me.
No, there's nothing I'd like less than to get
    together at your product launch reception.
No, I regret I can't squeeze your brunch into my schedule
    – you'll be notified should an opening occur.
No, I don't appear to have received an invitation
    to your barbecue – it must have gone astray.
No, my cellphone was out of range, my e-mail caught a virus,
    I had run out of notepads, parchment, discs, papyrus.
No, you can take No for an answer, without bothering
    your head to pop the question.
No, even Yes means No in my tongue, under my breath:
    No, absolutely not, not a snowball's chance, not a hope.

NOT YOURSELF

Monday, you take the accordion out of its case in rain,
                              begin to busk.
Tuesday, you complain that the raïto sauce with your hake
                              is far too garlicky.
Wednesday, you temp as a PA in a software solutions firm,
                              filing your cherry-red nails.
Thursday, you will be the youth arranging for his sailboard
                              to be tattooed with a nude.
Friday, you gain consciousness after your last-chance
                                             operation
                              to beat prostate cancer.

Monday, you will be a gate-leaning farmer, watching tall
                                             wheat
                              ripen like bamboo.
Tuesday, you are on duty at the beauty salon, adding
                                             volumising
                              shampoo to crestfallen hair.
Wednesday, you will be fitted with a spinal stimulator, if
                                             metabolic
                              complications are resolved.
Thursday, you are a salesman picking your teeth as you leave
                              a small-town hotel.
Friday, you try your damnedest to revive stalled peace
                                             negotiations
                              with your fellow-envoy.

Monday, you joke with other widows about the man who calls
                              the bingo numbers.
Tuesday, you are a parcel-lumbered motorcycle courier,
                              jousting with gridlock.
Wednesday, you will block the undertaker's lane, unloading
                              a consignment of veneer.

Thursday, you stack up cushions for a clearer view from the seat
of your adapted car.
Friday, you will attack defence computer systems worldwide
with your virus.

Monday, you bring the best case you can to the attention of
the sentencing review board.
Tuesday, you place yourself inside an orthopaedic corset to save
your back from strain.
Wednesday, your slow fast-lane driving is greeted with the kudos
of a two-finger salute.
Thursday, you know the acute pain of seeing the very twin of
your windcheater
at barely half the price.
Friday, you administer morphine to a doubly incontinent patient
in a dank public ward.

Monday, you will iron white shirts like a carpenter
planing a plank of deal.
Tuesday, you feel a cold coming on as you banter to your
passengers
on the tour coach.
Wednesday, you will broach the subject of a barring order
with your younger kids.
Thursday, you will change into uniform before collaring
your guard dog for patrol.
Friday, you will wake up stark naked, wearing only
your lover's arm.

Monday, you are a leotard-clad ballet dancer rehearsing
for *Coppelia* at the barre.
Tuesday, you are a car mechanic in a pit: dirt infiltrating skin,
grit irritating a graze.
Wednesday, you are the mindless old man whose happy release
his family prays for.

Thursday, you will give birth to a child, smuggled like a
                                        refugee
                    under your tarpaulin.
Friday, you will struggle across the fairway, humping your
                                        golf bag
                    like an oxygen tank.

Monday, either as a bank's investment analyst or flipping
                                        burgers
                    in a fast-food chain.
Tuesday, the unsame . . .

AT THE SEMINAR

I

An electronic blip from house-martins as they pass
an open window at the conference centre; frantic birds,
on errands of mercy, transporting relief supplies to tricorn beaks.
We sneak a glance at our mobiles for text messages.

Crawling across the hotel lawn, sun puts mist in the shade:
a transparent morning now, our vision unhindered for miles.
A golfing party, armed with a quiver of clubs, aims
for the bull's-eye of the first hole; others, near a pool
blue as our EU flag with its water sparkle of stars, dry off:
shrink-wrapped in towels, they sink back into resort chairs.

II

For serious objective reasons, we are informed, our keynote
speaker is delayed; the Chairman's interpreted words
are relayed simultaneously through headphones:
In order to proceed to a profitable guidance for our work
which will be carried out with a feature of continuity and priority . . .

I see the lake basking in its own reflected glory, self-absorbed,
imagine turquoise dragonflies, wings wide as wedding hats,
fish with scarlet fins, water-walking insects.

I intervene. I associate myself with the previous speaker's views.
Discussions go on in all our languages at once, as we unscrew
still mineral water, bottled at some local beauty spot.
Certain administrations suffered cuts as they weren't entrusted

with new attributions likely to fill in the logistical gap
resulting from the inference of the frontierless economic area . . .

In two hours (less, if – with luck – that stupid clock has
      stopped)
our final workshops will convene in the break-out rooms.
Then it will be time to draw conclusions at the plenary,
to score evaluation forms, return to our respective floors
to dress down for the bus tour of the Old Town.

III

Now the rapporteurs start synopsising
the workshop findings on felt-tip flip-charts.
The Chairman is summing up: *New challenges*
overlook the world scenery in our global stance . . .

Lily pads strut across the lake like stepping stones;
fish risk an upward plunge; martins – plucking
sustenance from thick air – lunge at their mud nests.
Hold the world right there. Don't move a single thing.

GERM WARFARE

As saints kissed lepers' sores, caressed rank beggars' wounds,
    I ought to thank God for the way you
    Spray me with your germs, my fellow travellers.
I should take it like a seraph, or at least like a man,

Ingest your pestilence with relish, meditate indulgently
    On sprinklers dousing a striped lawn,
    Feel proud to hothouse your viruses in my lungs,
Pick up stray bugs like hitchhikers, pets needing a good home.

So by all means go on sneezing in that spunky style of yours:
    The convulsion, the eruption, the paroxysm, the pile-drive,
    The dog yelp, the orgasm, the gale force, the squelch,
The caught short, the sudden brake, the snort, the screech owl.

Let it all hang out, therefore, whatever it happens to be.
    You with the unprotected schnoz, as though a hanky's
    Prophylactic would sin against your principles, your faith,
You who pass your plague around like cough drops,

You can be relied upon to prop yourself beside me
    On the bus, telling your cellphone how much
    You suffer, as you present me with hard evidence,
Certain that a problem shared is a problem halved.

The morning before the long plane journey, the crucial interview,
    The special date, whenever hoarseness begins to tighten
    Round my throat like a noose, thoughts wander back to you,
Eyes water, touched by the largesse with which you showered me,

Smitten to the core by your infectious charms. Bless you!

SO MUCH DEPENDS

The red barn. The Vermont farm
you fled from to the city
or vowed you'd retire to some day.

The barn at your grandparents'
in Kansas where you stowed away
one preteen summer, happy

to be left alone, at sea on the prairie,
hay spilling before cutter blades,
waves breaking on an inland shore.

A battened-down barn, holly-berry red
against the first dusting of snow.
Chevron-patterned wagon doors.

The grocery store forty miles off,
an upstate Amish village planted
among neat-drilled horse-tilled fields.

There will always be room
in the scheme of things for a red barn.
You may depend your life on it.

Inhale cured fodder, grain, manure.
Admit winter cattle to the stalls.
This is your clapboard cathedral:

pillars, nave, aisles, weather vane.
Wheat is separated from
chaff here, sheep from goats.

Come back, Grandma Moses, lead us
from the desert of downtown
to the promised land of the red barn.

TIME PIECES

I

How long a day lasts.
It starts at dawn,
goes on all night,
right into the small
hours, finds time
for each minute
individually, wastes
no second,
however swift.

II

How long days take.
An evening waiting
for the phone to ring
as if for a watched kettle
to come gasping
to the boil and sing.
A week in which your lover
mulls the situation over.
A summer marking time
before exam results.
The breathing space
the lab requires
to prove your GP
right or wrong.

III

The grandfather clock keeps
time under lock and key,
counts the seconds like a miser
inside walnut-panelled vaults.

Its chimes disturb light sleepers,
hold them in suspense
until another hour's demise
is hammered home.

IV

The word *forever* as used
in a pop song chorus.
The word *vintage* as it occurs
in the second-hand shop-talk
of the clothes store – say, in
this label: *Vintage Slip, 1980s.*

V

When we settled in
         to the new house,
distancing ourselves
         from our sour past,
secure at last in exultation,
         we knew we would
never again be as young
         as we were then;
nor had we been for years.

VI

         My contributor's copy
of *The New Younger Irish Poets*
         already liver-spotted with age.

VII

And to think
of her once-new
bijou town house –
sleek, chic, state-of-the-art,
latest in everything –
now being advertised for sale
'in need of modernisation'.

VIII

Seems only yesterday
you woke in this same
bedroom and dressed
for the same steady job,
here where you will wake
again for work tomorrow,
your yesterdays adding up
to thirty years of waking
since you were waved off
by hands it now takes
memory to flesh out.

IX

Like the snow in Joyce's story
that falls all over Ireland,
on the living and the dead,
grey hair has lodged
on most heads of my generation
and the first flurries start
to take root in the next.

X

December 31st: punch line to your diary.
The date when time runs out.
When you may take your case no farther.
When you must sign off, watching your
dead – in passé glasses, retro gabardines –
lag behind, as you place your faith blindly
in a new year's resolution of your plot.

XI

It comes almost as a relief,
the long-anticipated voice
creeping down the line:
the phone call you had
coming for a long time,
for years of nights;
a dark secret, a rodent
gnawing at your sleep.

XII

Travel as a backward step.
You journey until you find
a meadow where wildflowers
grow with pre-factory-farming
copiousness, a horse-drawn
landscape where hay is saved
in older ways, to revive
the life you lived once,
catch up with your past.

XIII

Whatever it was you feared
has not come to pass.
Not tonight at least.
Whatever it is afflicts you
will not last.

Your siege will lift.
You will take the risk
eventually to say,
'Things really were unbearable
way back then.'

XIV

How briefly a day
lasts, unravelling so fast
you can't keep pace.
You are at the morning
bus stop, wondering
if you definitely
locked the hall door
when, what seems
like seconds later,
sunset struts by
in all its sky-draped
finery, its evening
wear, and you are
unlocking the hall door.

XV

Wiping clean the day's dark slate,
sleep sweeps you off your feet,
leaves you dead to the world
in your bedclothes, shrouded in sheets.

Some new and recent poetry from Anvil

GAVIN BANTOCK
Just Think of It

PETER DALE
Under the Breath

DICK DAVIS
Belonging

HARRY GUEST
A Puzzling Harvest
COLLECTED POEMS 1955–2000

MICHAEL HAMBURGER
From a Diary of Non-Events

JAMES HARPUR
Oracle Bones

PHILIP HOLMES
Lighting the Steps

PETER LEVI
Viriditas

GABRIEL LEVIN
Ostraca

E A MARKHAM
A Rough Climate

SALLY PURCELL
Collected Poems

GRETA STODDART
At Home in the Dark

JULIAN TURNER
Crossing the Outskirts

DANIEL WEISSBORT
Letters to Ted